Savoring Chelan

Savoring Chelan

Pairing Local Wines with Regional Recipes

Compiled by Morgan Fraser

Travel
Addict
Publishing

For more information, contact:

Travel Addict Publishing
P.O. Box 1134
Chelan, WA 98816
info@savoringchelan.com

SavoringChelan.com

Back cover picture by Richard Uhlhorn.
Cover art by Kerry Siderius.
Cover design by Kasey Koski.

ISBN 978-0-9829566-0-1

Printed in the United States of America by InstantPublisher.com

For Nana

TABLE OF CONTENTS

Table of contents continues on following page

TABLE OF CONTENTS (CONTINUED)

FOREWORD

Welcome to *Savoring Chelan,* a cookbook that pairs Chelan Valley wines with local recipes.

This book was created to share my love of the Chelan Valley with readers drawn to the area for its beauty, climate, food and wines. The chefs, cooks and winemakers who contributed feel the same way as I do: that the Chelan Valley is a unique place and experience that should be celebrated as such.

Chelan is not just about wine. It is also about fresh fruit, fresh fish, locally-grown produce, a small-town feel, and enjoying the cool, pristine lake. Remove any one of these ingredients and you would not end up with the same result.

A few notes on the recipes and wine pairings:

When the recipe contributor has recommended a wine, the name of the wine is followed by an asterisk (*). Otherwise, the wine pairing recommendations are mine, with input from local winemakers.

The wine pairings are suggestions to give you an idea of what would go well with each of the dishes, and there is an index in the back of the book where you can cross-reference which recipes are listed with your favorite wines. However, they are by no means the only wines that pair with the dishes: pairing depends largely on personal taste, and while one person may completely agree with a wine pairing suggestion, another may prefer something else entirely. The beauty of the Chelan Valley is that there are wines for every palate: with a little bit of experimentation, you can find a recipe and a wine that will fit any occasion.

Savoring Chelan has something for everyone. The recipes appeal to a wide range of personal taste and are varying levels of difficulty, preparation and cook time. To try something new or find a new twist to an old favorite, simply peruse the recipes, pictures and commentary from the people who know the area's food and wine best.

If the recipe contributor is a winery owner, you will be directed to their winery page at the beginning of the book. Otherwise, you will find information about them in the contributor's section at the back.

In many cases, the recipe writers included recommendations on where to find ingredients locally. If you're not cooking in Chelan, you can usually find the item or something comparable at your local grocery store.

Enjoy!

Morgan Fraser, author, *Savoring Chelan*

INTRODUCTION

Although the Chelan Valley is relatively new to wine, it is by no means new to quality food using fresh and local ingredients. Most of the area that has become vineyard was originally orchard: apples, cherries and other soft fruits. Generations of families have grown produce in the area, and the growing wine industry simply means that more people can enjoy the valley's agriculture on site. Wine grapes have been planted in the valley for over a hundred years; quite a few acres were dedicated to juice grapes for the Welch's Juice Company more than 60 years ago.

The modern era of wines in the valley began with the Lake Chelan Winery in Manson, which opened its doors in 2002, followed by Wapato Point Cellars the following spring. Many others followed soon after. Now the Valley celebrates more than 15 wineries, tasting rooms and local vineyards, with more plantings and winery openings every day.

In 2009, Lake Chelan was granted status as an American Viticultural Area (AVA). An AVA is an area with unique climate, soil and physical characteristics that distinguish it from surrounding areas. What is produced within the AVA would not be the same grown somewhere else, a fact undoubtedly showcased in the wines created from Chelan Valley fruit.

Once a tourist area that drew visitors to the sunny hot summers and cool pristine lake, the Chelan Valley has now become a destination for families and individuals that also appreciate good glass of wine and a delicious meal in beautiful surroundings.

Savoring Chelan captures the spirit of the Chelan Valley: local chefs and cooks, winemakers and winery owners sharing their favorite recipes and wine pairings from the valley they know and love. You can enjoy many of these dishes at local restaurants and all of these wines during your visit to the valley, but you can also take the experience home with you and recreate a taste of Chelan in your own kitchen, as many times as you like, for years to come.

Shane Collins

President, Lake Chelan Wine Growers Association

Wineries

"Ripe and Sweet" by Kerry Siderius

Wineries

"Ripe and Sweet" by Kerry Siderius

ANTOINE CREEK VINEYARDS

Antoine Creek partners, left to right: Ed Haskell, Jeanie Haskell, Harold Thoreen and Suzanne Haggard.

Ed and Jeanie Haskell purchased an apple orchard on Highway 97 between Azwell Dam and the town of Pateros in 1998. Antoine Creek Vineyard came to fruition when the Haskells began replacing the trees with grapevines in 2002. Several years later, Harold Thoreen and Suzanne Haggard became partners in the venture.

The majority of grapes harvested at Antoine Creek are purchased by local wineries. The Viognier and Riesling grapes – the first varieties to be planted – are in great demand. Gewürztraminer has proven that it can produce a fabulous ice wine available at Rio Vista Winery, 2 miles south of the vineyard on the Columbia River.

Antoine Creek Vineyard also grows a special clone of Pinot Noir, and more recently has started cultivating Malbec and Cabernet Franc varieties. You can taste wine made from most of these grapes at Rio Vista. The 2008 vintage of Pinot Noir has proven to be exceptional and can be found at Vin du Lac Winery in Chelan.

C. R. Sandidge

A quarter of a century of winemaking experience in Europe and Washington State are represented in the wines crafted by C. R. Sandidge. In 2007, the 2002 Tri*Umph was rated the finest red wine produced in all of North America, Australia, New Zealand and South America in Jerry D. Mead's New World International Wine Competition. More than 50 Wine Spectator and Wine Enthusiast scores of 90 points or better have been awarded to the red, white and dessert wines crafted by their winemaker, Ray Sandidge III, with the highest score to date being an amazing 97 points. Visit their friendly tasting room in Manson and enjoy their Syrah, Viognier, red Bordeaux blends, red Rhone Valley blend, dry Rosé and dessert wine.

Photo by Richard Uhlhorn

C. R. Sandidge Wines
145 E. Wapato Way, Suite 1
Manson, WA
509.682.3704
crsandidgewines.com

FOUR LAKES WINERY

Four Lakes Winery is one of the newer wineries in the Chelan Valley. They make big, bold red wines that stand alone or can be paired with many foods. Their white wines are light and crisp, to be savored at the winery or at home on a hot day.

Four Lakes invites you to share their beautiful 360-degree view of Chelan, Wapato, Roses and Dry Lakes and the incredible Cascade Mountains at the tasting room in Manson. Their production facility is located on Howard Flats, perched high above the Columbia River; both have a view to remember year round! Contact them for a tour of the vineyard and get the chance to talk with owner Don Koester and winemaker Karl Koester — they would love for you to join them.

Four Lakes Winery
4491 Wapato Lake Road
Manson, WA
509.687.0726
fourlakeschelanwinery.com

HARD ROW to HOE

vineyards

In the late 1930's, when construction on Grand Coulee Dam started to wind down, some ladies that had been making a living there decided to move to the old Edgemont Lodge, located across the bay from Lucerne on Lake Chelan. The mine at Holden Village above Lucerne was in its heyday, and the ladies relocated to offer their professional services to the miners. Being as there was no road or trail from Lucerne to the lodge, an enterprising man from Manson started a rowboat taxi service shuttling the miners to the brothel.

Located at 300 Ivan Morse Road in Manson, the Hard Row to Hoe tasting room has assumed the décor of what might have been an old-time brothel parlor. Folks may come to see the décor, but they come back for the wine.

Hard Row to Hoe
300 Ivan Morse Road
Manson, WA
509.687.3000
hardrow.com

KARMA VINEYARDS

Photo by Richard Uhlhorn

Karma Vineyards, located on the sunny southern shore of Lake Chelan, invites you to visit and enjoy their many wines, as Karma is one of only three Methode Champenoise producers in the state of Washington. It's worth the visit to sample their exquisite tribute to this wine.

You can also enjoy the signature Karma Kafé, featuring chef Amilee Cappell Olson. Karma Vineyards believes that food and wine play a synonymous role in your experience at Karma, so come enjoy their one-of-a-kind food and wine pairing experience in the Karma underground wine cave.

Karma Vineyards
1681 S. Lakeshore Road
Chelan, WA
509.682.5538
goodkarmawines.com

LAKE CHELAN WINERY AND THE BBQ IN THE VINEYARD

Located in the last privately owned apple packing shed in the Valley, Lake Chelan Winery is the pioneer of the Lake Chelan Valley wine industry. The expansive grounds feature free tastings of their award-winning estate wines, a 3,000 square-foot gift shop, working vineyards and winery tours. Relax and enjoy their famous BBQ with a bottle of estate wine in the heart of the vineyard. Lake Chelan Winery shows appreciation to all of their customers by throwing the exciting parties and events, and is always family friendly.

The tasting room is open daily at 11 a.m. year-round. The BBQ in the Vineyard is open daily May through October.

Lake Chelan Winery and the BBQ in the Vineyard
SR 150 Chelan Manson Hwy
Chelan, WA
509.687.9463 (WINE)
lakechelanwinery.com

NEFARIOUS CELLARS

Photo by Charity Burggraaf

In 1998, Dean and Heather Neff planted a test block vineyard 20 minutes north of Lake Chelan at the bottom of the Methow Valley with Pinot Noir, Cabernet Sauvignon and everything in between.

In 2001, they headed to the Willamette Valley in Oregon to make Pinot Noir. Dean worked for Bud Beck at Advanced Vineyards, then moved on to make wine under Isabelle Dutarte at Deponte and Tony Soter and James Cahill at Soter Vineyards. Heather sold wines from relatively hard-to-find producers.

On the side, they started a label called Nonni and Zing. It was a small project of about 250 cases annually, and was made entirely from fruit sourced from the Dundee Hills AVA.

In 2004, Washington and its endless possibility lured them home. Dean and Heather found their property on the south shore of the Lake Chelan AVA and closed on it in June of that year.

That same year, they planted more vineyard near the original test block: Rocky Mother (Syrah) and Stone's Throw (Riesling). The following year was spent building the wine-making facility and planting Defiance, their on-site vineyard. The Nefarious Cellars tasting room opened for Valentine's Day 2006.

If you're in Chelan, Heather and Dean hope that you take a drive through their vineyard and climb their little slope; you'll like what you find at the top.

Nefarious Cellars
495 S. Lakeshore Road
Chelan, WA
509.682.9505
nefariouscellars.com

RIO VISTA WINES

"Rio Vista Beach with Jack" by Kerry Siderius

Rio Vista Wines, a small well-manicured estate winery, is slightly "off the beaten path," but often the path to some of the best wines is a little out of the way. Located on the banks of the beautiful Columbia River, Rio Vista is just 10 minutes north of Chelan and the only winery you can get to by boat, float plane or car.

You're sure to enjoy lingering in the golden glow of the river while sipping exquisite wines on the covered deck off the tasting room, on the new riverside deck, under the tiki-style hut or on the spacious lawns. A walk through the riverside vineyards, viewing the birds, boaters and fishermen from the sandy beach, or visiting the ducks and chickens may complete your visit.

The estate's award-winning wine varieties include Chardonnay, Riesling, Sunset on the River, Loony Red and Cabernet Sauvignon.

Rio Vista Wines
22415 Highway 97
Chelan, WA
509.682.9713
riovistawines.com
Open Wednesday to Sunday from noon to 6 p.m. June to October.
Open Friday to Sunday from noon to 5 p.m. November to May.
10 minutes north of Chelan on Hwy 97: Go 1/2 mile north of milepost
243, turn right at the mailboxes and follow the signs.
By boat: 8 miles north of the Beebe Bridge boat launch. Pull up onto the
west side of the sandy beach near the hut.
By plane: call Lake Chelan Sea Planes at 509.682.5555.

Tsillan
C E L L A R S

Tsillan Cellars is the crown jewel of the youthful, vibrant and rapidly growing Lake Chelan wine tourism scene. Tsillan Cellars, an Italian country winery recreated on the gently sloping shores of Lake Chelan, offers a destination experience unique in the entire country.

Three waterfalls form an amphitheater backdrop for the island stage. Natural stone bridges, natural slate terraces and walks, Tuscan stone columns, a 35-foot bell tower with a 650-pound bronze bell, landscaped rockeries and gardens all overlook Lake Chelan and the Cascade Mountains.

The 135-acre estate, with 36 acres dedicated to vineyards, is well on its way to receiving national recognition. The attention to the finest viticulture techniques has already produced numerous award-winning wines and a growing acceptance among wine connoisseurs.

The winery name is taken from a 19th century explorer who, upon hearing the native word for the lake, mapped it as "Tsillan," pronounced "Chelan" and meaning deep water.

Tsillan Cellars
3875 Highway 97A
Chelan, WA 98816
509.682.9463
tsillancellars.com

TUNNEL HILL WINERY AND SUNSHINE FARM

On the shores of Lake Chelan, in a cool, quiet cellar under the hillside, Tunnel Hill Winery creates handcrafted wines using age-old techniques. Made with the same patience and care as the landmark granite cottage that houses the winery, Tunnel Hill wines speak of the craftsmanship of another time, when attention to detail mattered and small artisans flourished.

Tunnel Hill is part of the Sunshine Farm, a diverse, 4th-generation family farm dedicated to supplying North Central Washington with the best in local fruits, organic vegetables, grass-fed beef, wine, and other artisan products. Denny Evans, his son Guy, and Guy's wife Rachel own the land and tend the tree fruit, wine grape,

Photo by Richard Uhlhorn

winery, vegetable, and farm market operations. Stop by and see them anytime.

Tunnel Hill Winery
509.682.3243
tunnelhillwinery.com

The Sunshine Farm Market
509.682.1350
thesunshinefarm.com
closed January to April

37 U.S. Highway 97A
Chelan, WA

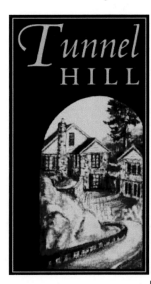

VIN DU LAC WINERY

The grounds surrounding the Vin du Lac winery have been orchard land since the 1920's, and half of the property remains a working orchard. Winemaker Larry Lehmbecker acquired the existing apple orchard and buildings in 2002. Seven acres of estate vineyard were planted that spring and designated "Michaela's Vineyard."

The winery was originally housed in two old orchard sheds that were fully remodeled and updated to serve as modern winery production facilities. Remnants of the buildings' former character remain, including the hand-laid stone foundation of the barrel room, which bears the inscription "Sept. 1937." The old orchard farmhouse, built in the 1920's, has also been updated, and now serves as the winery tasting room and bistro. In 2009 a state-of-the-art production facility was opened in Chelan Falls.

Larry is a long-time hobbyist brewer and winemaker, who has recently devoted himself to the study of formal, commercial winemaking; the results are evident in his Vin du Lac wines. Larry's travels to Provence and Paris over the years have also inspired and influenced him.

Vin du Lac currently produces 10000+ cases per year. The red wines are made from grapes coming primarily from the Sunnyside and Prosser areas of Yakima Valley. Estate and locally-grown Chelan area grapes comprise about 50 percent of the white wines here at Vin du Lac. The remaining 50 percent are from grapes grown in the Sunnyside and Horse Heaven Hills areas.

Our estate wines are designated with a black label and the name "Lehm," meaning "earth" or "loam" in German. It is also Larry's dad's nickname!

Vin du Lac/Chelan Wine Company
105 Highway 150
Chelan, WA
866.455.WINE
vindulac.com

WapatoPoint Cellars
& the Winemaker's Grill

Wapato Point Cellars wines are made with a clear focus on quality that begins in their local vineyards. Hand-picked and sorted, the cool climate of the valley lends itself to growing the perfect grapes to craft the exceptional wines served in their restaurant. Relax on the outdoor patio with a glass of award-winning estate wine, then step into the casual elegance of the Winemaker's Grill. Choose a great steak or a delicious item off the ever-changing fresh sheet. Come experience the warm hospitality and welcoming atmosphere of Wapato Point Cellars and the Winemaker's Grill.

The Wapato Point Cellars Tasting Room opens at noon; the Winemaker's Grill opens at 5 p.m. daily.

Wapato Point Cellars
200 Quetilquasoon Road
Manson, WA
509.687.4000
wapatopointcellars.com

Appetizers

"Apples to Grapes" by Kerry Siderius

Appetizers

"Apples to Grapes" by Kerry Siderius

APPLE CHEESE BREAD

This bread is best made with fresh Washington Fujis, which are picked in October. It goes great with homemade soup; see the soups and salads section on page 25.

Prep time: 15 minutes
Cook time: 50-60 minutes
Serves 8

see the soups and salads section on page 25.

> ### RECIPE TIP
> *If your apples are dry, add 1 Tbs. of water or the bread will be dry.*

- 2 eggs
- 1/2 cup butter
- 2/3 cup sugar
- 1 1/2 cups grated Fuji apples (about 2 large apples)
- 2 cups sifted flour
- 1 teaspoon baking powder
- 1/2 teaspoon baking soda
- 1/2 teaspoon salt
- 3/4 cup grated cheddar cheese
- 1/2 cup chopped walnuts or pecans

Preheat oven to 350°F and grease a 9"x5"x3" loaf pan. Beat the eggs, butter and sugar until fluffy. Stir in the apples, flour, baking powder, baking soda and salt. Add in the cheese and nuts.

Pour the mixture into a greased loaf pan. Bake for 50-60 minutes, or until the center of the loaf is firm.

Cool the bread for 5-10 minutes in the pan, then remove and cool on a wire rack. Although the bread is great warm, it will cut more easily if allowed to cool completely.

Contributed by Mary Weldy, co-owner of the Culinary Apple, page 88.

Pairs well with:
C.R. Sandidge Winery KISS Chardonnay Gewürtzraminer Blend
Vin du Lac Les Amis White Blend
Wapato Point Cellars Sauvignon Blanc

CORIANDER AND CILANTRO FLATBREAD WITH OLIVE CHOP

Prep time: 35 minutes
Cook time: 5 minutes
Serves 4

Olive Chop
- 1 cup Kalamata olives, pitted
- 1/4 cup capers
- 1 tablespoon lemon zest
- 1/4 cup parsley

Flatbread
- 1 1/2 cups (or more) unbleached all purpose flour
- 2 1/2 teaspoons ground coriander
- 1 1/2 teaspoons baking powder
- 3/4 teaspoon salt
- 1/2 teaspoon baking soda
- 1/3 cup chopped cilantro
- 3/4 cup (or more) Greek yogurt or plain whole milk yogurt
- Olive oil or non-stick spray

For the olive chop, place all ingredients in a blender or food processor and blend until coarsely chopped.

For the flatbread, sift flour, coriander, baking powder, salt and baking soda into a medium bowl. Stir in cilantro. Add yogurt and stir with fork until small clumps form. Knead the mixture in a bowl, just until the dough holds together, adding more flour or yogurt by the tablespoon until you form a soft and slightly sticky dough. Turn dough out onto a floured surface. Knead just until smooth; about 1 minute.

Divide dough into 8 equal pieces. Roll each piece into a ball and roll each ball out on floured surface until it's about 4-1/2 inches across. It's homemade; it doesn't have to be perfectly round! Brush with olive oil or spray with a non-stick spray. Grill each side on medium-high heat for 2 to 3 minutes. Remove from heat and serve with olive chop.

Contributed by Amilee Cappell Olson, chef at Karma Kafé, page 84.

Pairs well with:
*Karma Vineyards Estate Gewürztraminer**
*Karma Vineyards Methode Champenoise**
Wapato Point Cellars Kludt Family Reserve Merlot

FOUR LAKES FRESH SALSA

Prep time: 30 minutes
Marinating time: 12 hours (optional)
Serves 10

RECIPE TIP
Control the heat of your salsa with the jalapeño seeds. The more you put in, the hotter the salsa.

- 6 large diced tomatoes
- 1/2 cup diced garlic
- 1 diced jalapeño
- 1/2 cup chopped cilantro
- 3/4 cup chopped onions
- 1/4 cup chopped leeks
- 1/4 cup chopped scallions
- 2 cups chopped cabbage
- Juice from two limes
- 1-1/2 tablespoons salt
- Dash of pepper

Mix all ingredients together in large bowl. Add any other of your favorite fruits or vegetables, such as carrots, peaches or nectarines.

Serve fresh or let sit overnight in the refrigerator to let the flavors come together.

Serve with chips or tostadas.

Contributed by Karl Koester, winemaker at Four Lakes Winery, page 7.

Pairs well with:
Four Lakes Winery Chardonnay*
Hard Row to Hoe Edelzwicker Gewürtztraminer Riesling Blend
Tunnel Hill Estate Riesling

TERRIE'S FAMOUS HUMMUS WITH A KICK

Prep time: 5 minutes
Serves 4

- 1 can garbanzo beans (16 oz.)
- 2 tablespoons Tahini
- 3 cloves garlic
- 1 tablespoon honey
- 1/8 teaspoon or less African cayenne pepper
- Small bunch cilantro

RECIPE TIPS
- ✦ *Try substituting peanut butter for Tahini.*
- ✦ *Take the green growth out of the center of the garlic clove; it makes it bitter.*

Open the can of garbanzo beans, pour out half the liquid, and put the rest in food processor. Add Tahini, garlic, honey and African cayenne; blend until smooth and creamy. Throw a handful of fresh cilantro in at the end for taste and color.

Serve with crudités or baked pita chips, in wraps with fresh tomatoes and arugula, or with the Souvlaki on page 66.

Contributed by Terrie Holm-Nielsen, co-owner and designer at Columbia Furniture, page 86.

Pairs well with:
Tsillan Cellars Estate Pinot Grigio
Vin du Lac Grisant! Pinot Gris
Wapato Point Cellars Chelan Nouveau Beaujolais Nouveau

NOTES

Soups and Salads

"Grapes with Yellow Leaf" by Kerry Siderius

Soups and Salads

"Grapes with Yellow Leaf" by Kerry Siderius

ASIAN SALAD

Prep Time: 45 minutes
Serves 4

Salad
- 5 cups mixed salad greens
- 1 cup cooked shrimp
- 1 Jonagold, Pink Lady or Fuji apple, cored and diced
- 1 can sliced water chestnuts
- 1 cup bean sprouts
- 1/2 cup diced radishes
- 2 peeled and sliced carrots
- 2 stalks diced celery
- 1 cup chow mein noodles

Dressing
- 1/4 cup seasoned rice wine vinegar
- 2 teaspoons sugar
- 1/2 cup olive oil

RECIPE TIP
- *For best results, use fresh salad greens and apples that are in season.*
- *For fruit harvesting dates, see page 95.*

Submerge the salad greens in bowl of clean cold water. Drain the greens with a colander, wrap them in a paper towel and put them in a plastic bag. Refrigerate for at least 30 minutes to crisp the greens.

To make the dressing, combine the vinegar and sugar and whisk the olive oil into the mixture.

Toss all of the ingredients except the chow mein noodles in a large bowl and mix in the dressing. Top the salad with chow mein noodles.

Recipe contributed by Terrie Holm-Nielsen, co-owner and designer for Columbia Furniture, page 86.

Pairs well with:
Hard Row to Hoe Sauvignon Blanc
Lake Chelan Winery Gewürtzraminer
Vin du Lac "LEHM" Dry Riesling

ASIAN SOUP

Like most families, we were always busy raising kids and working. I wanted some easy tasty soups, so I came up with this recipe. It is especially fast if you make it using leftover rice and some sort of meat.

Prep Time: 7 minutes
Cook Time: 7 minutes
Serves 4

- 3 cups water
- 2 tablespoons bouillon
- 1 cup cooked rice (wild rice works well)
- 1 cup cubed cooked chicken, beef, fish or pork
- 1 cup frozen peas
- 1 cup assorted other vegetables (can be frozen, stir fry mix is good)
- 1/2 jar Sweet Red Chili Sauce

RECIPE TIP
"Better than Bouillon" is a great staple that can be kept in your fridge. Use chicken bouillon if you are using chicken leftovers, beef for beef leftovers and vegetable bouillon for fish or pork.

Bring water to boil and add bouillon. Bring back to a boil, add the rice, meat, peas, other vegetables and chili sauce. Heat for an additional 3-4 minutes and serve.

Contributed by Terrie Holm-Nielsen, co owner and designer at Columbia Furniture, page 86.

Pairs well with:
Lake Chelan Winery Chardonnay
Karma Vineyards Methode Champenoise
Vin du Lac Grisant! Pinot Gris

CLAMS HOSTETLER

Prep time: 5 minutes
Cook time: 5-10 minutes
Serves 4

- 1/4 cup olive oil
- 2 tablespoons butter
- 3 slices diced proscuitto
- 1/4 cup chopped leeks
- 8 cloves garlic, peeled and chopped
- 1 cup Four Lakes Riesling
- Juice of one small lime
- Dash of red pepper
- Salt and pepper
- 2 pounds manila or butter clams
- 1/3 cup Italian parsley, chopped

In a large frying pan, simmer olive oil, butter, prosciutto, leeks and garlic for 5 minutes. Add the Riesling, lime juice, and salt and pepper to taste.

Rinse clams, throwing away any that are already open, and add the rest to the broth.

Cover and simmer for 5 to 7 minutes or until all clams have opened. Sprinkle with fresh parsley and serve in small bowls with your favorite crusty bread to soak up the broth.

Contributed by Karl Koester, winemaker at Four Lakes Winery, page 7.

Pairs well with:
Four Lakes Winery Estate Riesling*
Hard Row to Hoe Viognier
Vin du Lac Barrel Select Chardonnay

EASY MINESTRONE SOUP

This easy soup is just bursting with the flavor of fresh vegetables, which can be varied depending on what is seasonally available. If time allows, substitute fresh veggies for canned. My 11 grandchildren clamor for me to make this. What better way for them to get their vegetables?

Prep Time: 30 minutes
Cook Time: 20 minutes
Serves 12

- 2 pounds ground beef
- 1 large onion (about 1 cup), chopped
- 2 cloves garlic, finely chopped
- 1 can (28 oz.) whole tomatoes
- 1 can (15 oz.) kidney beans
- 1 can (12 oz.) whole-kernel corn
- 2 stalks celery (about 1 cup), sliced
- 2 cups shredded cabbage (about 1/4 head)
- 2 small zucchini (about 2 cups), sliced
- 1/2 cup uncooked elbow macaroni or broken spaghetti
- 3 cups water
- 1/2 cup red wine or water
- 2 teaspoons instant beef bouillon
- 1-1/2 teaspoons salt
- 3-1/2 teaspoons Italian seasoning
- Freshly grated Parmesan cheese for topping

RECIPE TIPS

✦ *After browning beef, stir in all ingredients except macaroni, cover and refrigerate. 20 minutes before serving, add macaroni and continue cooking.*

✦ *Substitute any fresh or favorite vegetables that are in season, such as asparagus or carrots.*

✦ *To make breadsticks to go with the soup, cut a loaf of French bread in half, then into 4-inch long pieces. Cut each piece into 3 sticks. Brush cut sides with melted butter and sprinkle with Parmesan cheese. Bake sticks on ungreased pan at 450 ˚F until golden brown, about 8 minutes. Makes 30 bread sticks.*

Cook and stir ground beef, onion and garlic in Dutch oven or skillet until beef is light brown; drain. Stir in tomatoes (with liquid), kidney beans (with liquid) and remaining ingredients; break up tomatoes with fork.

Heat to boiling; reduce to medium heat. Cover and simmer, stirring occasionally, until macaroni and vegetables are tender, about 10 minutes.

Serve in large soup bowls topped with grated Parmesan cheese.

Contributed by Jan Little, co-owner of Rio Vista Wines, page 12.

Pairs well with:
*Rio Vista Estate Cabernet Sauvignon**
Lake Chelan Winery Merlot
Karma Vineyards Try Red Blend

FRUIT SALSA SALAD

Prep time: 30 minutes
Serves 6

Fruit Salsa
- 1/2 cup chopped sweet onion
- 2 tablespoons chopped cilantro
- 2 medium diced Fuji apples
- 2 cups blueberries
- 1 fresh orange, peeled, sectioned and cut into small pieces

Dressing
- 1/4 teaspoon salt
- 2 tablespoons sugar
- 2 tablespoons extra virgin olive oil
- 3 tablespoons apple juice
- 1/3 cup red wine vinegar

Garnish
- 1 1/4 cups mixed baby salad greens
- 1/2 cup crumbled Gorgonzola cheese

Gently stir all fruit salsa ingredients together.

Whisk dressing ingredients together, pour over the salad and let stand for 10 minutes.

Divide the greens onto 6 chilled plates, spoon fruit salsa over salad greens and top with cheese.

Contributed by Mary Weldy, co-owner of the Culinary Apple, page 88.

Pairs well with:
CR Sandidge Winery KISS Chardonnay Gewürtzraminer Blend
Karma Vineyards Methode Champenoise
Wapato Point Cellars Riesling

Karma's Green Goddess Dressing

Prep time: 15 minutes
Serves 8

RECIPE TIP
If substituting dried herbs for fresh, use 1/3 as much.

- 1/4 cup Greek yogurt or plain yogurt
- 2 cups mayonnaise
- 1/4 cup fresh parsley
- 1/4 cup fresh thyme
- 1/4 cup fresh tarragon
- 1/4 cup fresh-squeezed lemon juice
- 1/2 tablespoon raw sugar
- 2 shallots, peeled and chopped in half
- 2 cloves garlic, peeled and crushed

Put all ingredients in blender or food processor and blend until smooth. Serve over your favorite salad greens. The dressing will keep for up to two weeks in the refrigerator.

Contributed by Amilee Cappell Olson, chef at Karma Kafé, page 84.

Pairs well with:
*Karma Vineyards Estate Gewürztraminer**
*Karma Vineyards Methode Champenoise**
Four Lakes Winery Sauvignon Blanc

LOCAL MYTH GREEK SALAD

Prep time: 20 minutes
Set time: 12 hours (optional)
Serves 6-8

Dressing
- 2 teaspoons Worcestershire sauce
- 1 teaspoon Dijon mustard
- 1/2 teaspoon sea salt
- 1/2 teaspoon whole black peppercorns
- 1/4 cup mayonnaise
- 2 teaspoons fresh-squeezed lemon juice
- 1-2 cloves of garlic
- 3/4 cup extra virgin olive oil

Salad
- 8 cups romaine hearts (a family-sized bag)
- 1/3 cup Kalamata olives, pitted and torn into pieces, or wedges
- 1/3 cup red onion, cut into quarters and sliced thin
- 1/3 cup Feta cheese
- 1/2 cup Roma tomatoes, thinly sliced, or halved cherry tomatoes
- 1 teaspoon toasted pine nuts (see recipe tips for toasting directions)
- Pepperoncini peppers for garnish

> ### RECIPE TIPS
> ✦ Feta cheese is a style, not an animal; Local Myth uses domestic Feta from cow milk. Sheep or goat feta can also be used.
> ✦ To toast pine nuts, preheat oven to 350°F. Bake for 3-5 minutes in a single layer. Check often; they burn easily.

Put all dressing ingredients except for the olive oil in a blender and mix well. Slowly add the olive oil to emulsify the dressing (to make it thick and creamy.) If it comes out runny, you have 'broken' it. The dressing will still taste okay, but the creamy look and feel is lost.

For best results, refrigerate the dressing overnight and add more olive oil if needed.

Wash, dry, and chill the romaine hearts for 10 minutes before cutting them into large pieces. Put the cut romaine in a mixing bowl and add the dressing. Add olives, red onion, feta and tomatoes. Toss the salad until thoroughly coated with dressing. Garnish with pepperoncinis and pine nuts.

Contributed by Art Sill, co-owner of Local Myth Pizza, page 87.

Pairs well with:
Four Lakes Winery Sauvignon Blanc
Vin du Lac Les Amis White Blend
Vin du Lac Savvy Blanc

Long Beach Clam Chowder

This is a clam chowder recipe that we made with Razor clams from the Washington Coast when we had John and Jan Little of Rio Vista Wines for dinner. It goes well with their white wines that use our grapes.

Prep time: 45 minutes
Cook time: 20 minutes
Serves 10-12

- 1/2 pound diced slab bacon
- 2 tablespoons unsalted butter
- 2 large onions, peeled and diced
- 1/4 cup flour
- 2 cups clam broth, or 2 jars (2 cups) clam nectar
- 4 pounds diced potatoes
- 1 1/2 teaspoons dried thyme
- Ground pepper
- 24-32 cleaned Razor clams, coarsely chopped
- 2 cups milk
- 2 cups heavy cream or whipping cream
- 3 tablespoons chopped Italian parsley

Cook bacon in soup pot over low heat until wilted and slightly browned. Add butter and onions; cook until onions turn clear. Add flour and cook another 5 minutes. Add the broth, potatoes, thyme, and pepper. Simmer until potatoes can be easily pierced with fork but are still firm, adding more water as needed for preferred consistency (up to 2 cups).

Add the clams and bring the mixture back to a simmer. Add the milk and cream. Stir constantly over very low heat until the soup is hot but not boiling; if it boils the soup will curdle. Serve immediately, topped with fresh parsley.

Contributed by Jeanie Haskell of Antoine Creek Vineyards, page 5.

Pairs well with:
Rio Vista Viognier (Antoine Creek Vineyards)*
Hard Row to Hoe Primitivo
Tsillan Cellars Estate Pinot Grigio

Mexican Soup

Raising kids and working full time, I needed fast and healthy soups for the winter. I created this delicious soup out of that need. Enjoy!

Prep time: 7 minutes
Cook time: 7 minutes
Serves 4

- 3 cups water
- 2 tablespoons bouillon
- 1 can (16 oz.) hominy
- 1 small can tomatillo salsa verde
- 1 cup cooked chicken or beef, chopped
- 1 can (12 oz.) Mexican stewed tomatoes
- 1 cup grated sharp cheddar cheese
- Tortilla chips for garnish

> ### RECIPE TIP
> *"Better than Bouillon" is a great staple that can be kept in your fridge. Use chicken boullion if you are using chicken leftovers, beef for beef leftovers and vegetable bullion for fish or pork.*

Bring water to boil and add bouillon. Bring back to a boil, add the hominy, salsa, meat, and tomatoes. Heat for an additional 3-4 minutes until the soup simmers. Ladle the soup into bowls, top with grated cheese and serve with tortilla chips.

Contributed by Terrie Holm-Nielsen, co-owner and designer at Columbia Furniture, page 86.

Pairs well with:
Hard Row to Hoe Syrah
Tsillan Cellars Columbia Valley Piccolo Rosso
Vin du Lac Les Amis White Blend

SPICY TOMATO SOUP

I love this tomato soup because of my need to use the large amount of tomatoes coming out of my garden. Every year I plant more tomatoes than I need, leaving me an abundance that have found a home in this recipe.

Prep time: 15 Minutes
Cook time: 1.5 Hours
Serves up to 8

- 12-15 fresh garden tomatoes (about 3 pounds)
- 1 small can tomato paste
- Olive oil
- Tapatio, or your favorite hot sauce
- Salt and pepper
- 1/4 cup butter
- 2 large shallots or half a red onion, finely diced
- 4 cups chicken stock
- 1 cup cream or whole milk
- Fresh garden basil

RECIPE TIPS

- ✦ Using an immersion blender makes this recipe a breeze.
- ✦ You can skip roasting the tomatoes by substituting canned stewed tomatoes.
- ✦ Ripe, locally grown produce greatly improves the quality of this dish.

Preheat oven to 400°F. Start your largest pot boiling with water. Score the bottom of the tomatoes and drop in boiling water for 15-20 seconds, followed by a minute or so in cold ice water. Remove from ice bath and peel off skins. Cut in half and place cut side up on a rack and baking sheet to go in oven. Drizzle each tomato with olive oil, a shake or two of salt and pepper, and a good dash of your hot sauce, depending on your preferred level of heat; you can also add more later. Roast the tomatoes for about an hour. Remove and let cool.

While the tomatoes are cooking, begin heating a large pot; I prefer a 7-quart Dutch oven. Sauté shallots for a few minutes until they begin to turn translucent, then add tomato paste and stir for a few more minutes. Add chicken stock and cream, bring to a boil, reduce heat and simmer for about 10 minutes. Add roasted tomatoes and cook for a few more minutes.

Transfer to a large food processor or use an immersion blender and blend until smooth. For those who like a creamier texture, run the soup through a strainer.

Ladle into bowls, garnish with a lot of fresh basil and serve.

Contributed by Shane Collins, winemaker Tsillan Cellars Winery, page 85.

Pairs well with:
Tsillan Cellars Gewürztraminer*
Tsillan Cellars Off-Dry Riesling*

WINEMAKER'S WINTER STEW

Prep time: 30 minutes
Cook time: 1.5 hours
Serves 8-10

- 2-2/3 cups water
- 1 can kidney beans
- 1 can pinto beans
- 1 can garbanzo beans
- 2 cans stewed tomatoes or 3 large fresh tomatoes, peeled
- 1 large onion, chopped
- 3 bay leaves
- 4 bouillon cubes
- 2 stalks celery, chopped
- 3 sprigs fresh Oregano
- 1 pound ground beef or steak, cooked and drained
- 1/2 small cabbage, loosely chopped
- 2 carrots, chopped into medallions
- 1 medium potato, cubed
- 4 large basil leaves, chopped
- 1/4 bunch cilantro, chopped
- 1 teaspoon pepper
- 1 teaspoon salt
- 2 cloves garlic, diced
- 2 teaspoons crushed red pepper
- Juice from 1 lime
- 1 small zucchini, chopped into medallions
- 1/3 cup Four Lakes Cabernet Sauvignon

Using a 4-quart stock pot, bring water, kidney, pinto and garbanzo beans, tomatoes, onions and bay leaves to a boil. Reduce heat, cover and simmer for 20 minutes. Stir in bouillon, celery, oregano, and beef, simmering for 15 minutes. Add the cabbage and carrots. Simmer until carrots are tender, about 10-15 minutes. Add potato, cilantro, basil, garlic, pepper, salt, lime juice, red pepper and salt; simmer for 15 minutes. Finally, add the zucchini and wine, simmering until tender, about 10 to 15 minutes.

Contributed by Karl Koester, winemaker at Four Lakes Winery, page 7.

Pairs well with:
Four Lakes Winery Cabernet Sauvignon*
Rio Vista Estate Winery Cabernet Franc
Wapato Point Cellars Kludt Family Winery Reserve Merlot

NOTES

Entrees

"Cherries: Five Red Bing" by Kerry Siderius

Entrees

"Cherries: Five Red Bing" by Kerry Siderius

BAKED OR BARBECUED LAKE TROUT

While my "non-local" clients and fishing partners rave about the eating quality of our Mackinaw, I continue to hear local residents complain about their texture and taste. There are a few things you can do to ensure that your fish taste as good as they can: keep the fish cold, scrape off the loose body fat and don't overcook them. Beyond that, it's up to personal taste and expectations.

Prep time: 15 minutes
Cook time: 20-40 minutes, depending on the size of the fish
Serves 2-6

- 1 cleaned Mackinaw trout
- Salt and pepper
- 1 tablespoon dried basil or 3 tablespoons fresh basil, chopped
- Sliced onion OR sliced apple

> *RECIPE TIPS*
> *When picking a fresh Mackinaw for the barbecue, I look for the darkest flesh. Shrimp-fed, red-meat fish are the best tasting. Size doesn't matter, color does.*

Sprinkle salt and pepper and basil in the body cavity. Add a few slices of onion or apple. Wrap the fish in an aluminum foil envelope.

Place on the barbecue. A small fish of 2 to 3 pounds will need to barbecue about 10 to 12 minutes per side on low heat. Four- to 5-pound fish need about 15 minutes per side on low heat. Six- to 7-pound fish need about 17 to 19 minutes per side on low heat. The same formula works in the oven at about 350°F.

Serve with green salad, potato or rice side dish and a white or rosé wine.

Contributed by Anton Jones of Darrell & Dad's Family Guide Service, page 85.

Pairs well with:
Lake Chelan Winery Pinot Noir Rosé
Nefarious Cellars Viognier Defiance Vineyard Lake Chelan AVA
Rio Vista Winery Estate Riesling

BROILED COLUMBIA RIVER WILD CHINOOK SALMON

This recipe has been a family favorite for more than 30 years. I've tried other barbecued and baked salmon recipes over the years, but always come back to this one. It's one of the most requested fish recipes in our family and is now being passed along to a third generation.

Prep Time: 10 minutes
Marinating time: 30-90 minutes
Cook Time: 10 minutes per inch of thickness
Serves 4-6

- About 4 pounds 1 to 1-1/2 inch thick fillet of Columbia River salmon

Marinade
- Soy sauce, about 1/4 cup
- Lemon pepper, added after fish is marinated

Basting Sauce
- 1/2 cup soy sauce
- 1 cube butter

> ### RECIPE TIPS
> ✦ Substitute Columbia River salmon with Lake Chelan Lake trout, Rufus Woods Triploid trout, or Columbia River Steelhead.
> ✦ The season for Columbia River Chinook salmon opens in July.
> ✦ Contact local fishing guides if you need help catching one of these beauties.
> ✦ Visit Rio Vista and try our fantastic Columbia River smoked salmon and smoked cheese.

Sprinkle a generous amount of soy sauce on the flesh side of fillet. Add additional soy sauce as it is absorbed. Marinate in the refrigerator for 30-90 minutes. If short of time, make fork holes in the flesh to aid absorption.

Remove the marinated fillet from the refrigerator, place on broiling pan and sprinkle liberally with lemon pepper.

To make the basting sauce, melt a cube of butter in a small saucepan or in the microwave and blend 50/50 with soy sauce until smooth. Baste the salmon on the meat side with the blended sauce and then broil, skin side down, about 4 inches from the top oven element. A good rule for cooking fish is 10 minutes per inch of thickness. Check the fish every 2 to 3 minutes and continue to baste. A brown, bubbly crust will form. DO NOT OVERCOOK! When it can be easily flaked with a fork, it's done.

Contributed by John Little, co-owner and winemaker at Rio Vista Wines, page 12.

Pairs well with:
Rio Vista Estate Chardonnay*
Rio Vista's Loony Red (Yes, we recommend a red wine with this fish.)*
Lake Chelan Winery Pinot Noir Rosé

CAMPBELL'S FIRE PASTA

This is a local favorite that has been on more than a few Chelan restaurant menus over the years. The original recipe comes from former Campbell's chef, Duane Collette. Cooks being cooks, we started tinkering with it, just to eat something new. A few noodles, some freshly shredded Parmesan cheese, and Fire Pasta turned into a local culinary legend.

Prep time: 15 minutes
Cook time: 15 minutes
Serves 4

- One 12 oz. package pasta, preferably fettuccini or linguini
- 1/4 cup olive oil
- 3 cups chicken (1 pound), cut into 2-inch strips
- 1 teaspoon salt
- 2 teaspoons pepper
- 3/4 cup Worcestershire sauce
- 1-1/4 cups Frank's hot sauce
- 3 cups heavy whipping cream
- 1 tablespoon and 1 teaspoon red chili flakes

Hotel butter: whip the following ingredients until doubled in volume
- 2 tablespoons softened butter
- 1/4 teaspoon lemon juice
- 1 clove fresh minced garlic
- Pinch salt and pepper

Garnish
- Parmesan
- Parsley

> ### RECIPE TIP
> *To make the sauce spicier, add the red chili flakes to the pan during the deglazing process. Cooking the flakes will release their spicy flavor.*

Prepare pasta according to package directions. While it's cooking, sauté olive oil, chicken, salt and pepper in a pan until the chicken is browned on both sides. Remove the chicken from the pan; set aside. To deglaze, add the Worcestershire and hot sauce to the pan with the leftover oil; mix all ingredients until hot and blended. Add in the whipping cream and red chili flakes and add the chicken to finish cooking. Simmer the mixture until it is reduced into a thick sauce; adding 2 tablespoons of Parmesan will quicken the process. Drain the cooked pasta and toss with hotel butter first, then add in the sauce. Garnish with Parmesan and parsley.

Recipe contributed by Troy Nesvacil, chef at Campbell's Resort, page 87.

Pairs well with:
Hard Row to Hoe Pinot Gris
Rio Vista Estate Winery Chardonnay
Wapato Point Cellars Red Delicious

CARIBBEAN PORK TENDERLOIN

Prep time: 20 minutes
Marinade time: 1-2 hours
Cook time: 10 minutes
Serves 4

- Two whole pork tenderloins

Marinade
- 1/2 white onion, chopped
- 2 tablespoons minced garlic
- 1/2 cup fresh cilantro, chopped
- 2 teaspoons ginger powder
- 1-1/2 teaspoons dried oregano
- 1/2 teaspoon nutmeg
- 1/2 teaspoon cinnamon
- 3 tablespoons lemon juice
- 3 tablespoons soy sauce
- 6 tablespoons olive oil
- 1 teaspoon salt
- 2 tablespoons Balsamic vinegar

Sauté items
- 4 tablespoons butter
- 4 tablespoons brown sugar
- 2 whole apples, cored and cut into rounds (4 rounds per serving)
- 1 large sweet potato, peeled and cut into rounds (4 rounds per serving)

Garnish
- Fresh chopped cilantro
- Chopped pecans
- Olive oil
- Chopped green onion

Mix marinade items in a large glass or stainless steel mixing bowl. Cut pork tenderloins into 1 to 1-1/2 inch medallions and toss pork in the marinade until well coated. Refrigerate, covered, for 1 to 2 hours.

Remove pork medallions from marinade and grill 8 to 10 minutes, turning once. Sauté the apple and sweet potato slices in the butter with the brown sugar until lightly browned and softened.

Alternating sweet potato, pork, apple, sweet potato, pork and apple, make two stacks on the plate; you may need toothpicks. Garnish with cilantro, pecans, olive oil, green onion and serve with salad greens. Serve hot.

Contributed by Ray Sandidge, winemaker at C.R. Sandidge Wines, page 6.

Pairs well with:
C. R. Sandidge Dry Rosé of Pinot Noir*
C. R. Sandidge Stone Tree Red*

Chicken Skewers with Peanut Sauce

This is a dish I love to do early in the summer when my garden cilantro is at its peak.

Prep time: 15 Minutes
Cook time: 10 Minutes
Serves 4

Peanut sauce
- 1 cup natural peanut butter
- 1/2 cup chicken stock
- 1 lime
- 1 pinch cayenne pepper
- 1 tablespoon local honey
- Salt and pepper

Skewers:
- 4 chicken breasts; about 2 pounds
- 2 tablespoons peanut oil
- 4 drops sesame oil
- 2 tablespoons ginger infused soy sauce
  OR 2 tablespoons soy sauce and 2 teaspoons ginger
- Skewers (pre-soaked in water for 20 minutes)
- 1 cup fresh chopped cilantro

> ### Recipe Tips
> ✦ Local honey makes a world of difference.
> ✦ Don't skip the cilantro, it adds loads of flavor.
> ✦ Cook chicken on a baking sheet with a wire rack if you don't have an outdoor grill.

Preheat outdoor grill. Combine peanut butter, chicken stock, the juice from 1 lime, cayenne pepper, and honey in a small saucepan and bring to a simmer over medium heat. Stir occasionally. Combine peanut oil, sesame oil and ginger soy sauce in a small bowl and let flavors meld. Cut chicken into strips and place in a large bowl. Combine chicken strips with the peanut oil, sesame oil and soy sauce mixture and toss until chicken is well covered. Skewer chicken tenders and brush with the remaining oil mixture from the bottom of bowl for added flavor. Grill chicken until browned on both sides and cooked through. Remove from grill and garnish with fresh cilantro. Serve with peanut sauce.

Recipe contributed by Shane Collins, winemaker at Tsillan Cellars Winery, page 85.

Pairs well with:
Tsillan Cellars Estate Chardonnay*
Tsillan Cellars Estate Riesling*
Vin du Lac Savvy Blanc

FARM FRESH MEATLOAF

This is one of our favorite comfort suppers on a cold winter night. The recipe uses vegetables that are in season throughout the winter: onions and garlic, carrots and celeriac, which are harvested in late autumn and keep in the fridge for months. We also use grass-fed beef and dried herbs from our farm.

Prep time: 15 minutes
Cook time: 1 hour 15 minutes
Serves 6

- 2 tablespoons olive oil
- 1/2 small onion, finely chopped (about 1/2 cup)
- 1/2 medium celeriac, diced (about 1/2 cup)
- 1 large carrot, diced (about 1/2 cup)
- 2 large cloves garlic, minced
- 2 teaspoons dried parsley
- 1 teaspoon dried oregano
- 1 teaspoon dried sage
- 1 tablespoon dried basil
- 1-1/2 teaspoons salt
- 1 teaspoon dried mustard
- 1/2 teaspoon black pepper
- 1 large egg, beaten
- 2/3 cup milk
- 1/2 cup uncooked oatmeal
- 2 pounds ground beef
- 1/2 cup ketchup or barbecue sauce

RECIPE TIPS

- ✦ Celeriac is also known as celery root. It's a root crop related to celery, but it's much easier to grow and stores for months. It adds great celery flavor to soups, stews, and meatloaf.
- ✦ Oatmeal makes a great substitute for bread crumbs in any meatloaf recipe. It's less processed and healthier.
- ✦ For even greater flavor, substitute seasonal fresh herbs for the dried herbs (if substituting, use 3 times as much fresh herb).
- ✦ Pair this recipe with a side of sautéed collard greens—a great substitute for salad in the off-season. Strip leaves from stems, chop roughly, and sauté for about 5 minutes in olive oil. Add a little salt and enjoy!

Preheat the oven to 350°F. Heat olive oil in a heavy skillet. Saute onion, celeriac, and carrot over medium-high heat for about 5 minutes, until vegetables are tender and onions are golden. Add garlic and sauté 30 seconds more. Remove from heat and add parsley, oregano, sage, basil, dry mustard, salt, and pepper. In a large bowl, combine egg, milk, and oatmeal. Add ground beef and sautéed vegetables and mix thoroughly. Spoon into a loaf pan and cover with ketchup or barbecue sauce. Bake for 1 hour and 15 minutes, or until internal temperature reaches 160 degrees. Let rest 5 minutes before slicing and serving.

Contributed by Rachel Evans of Sunshine Farm, page 14.

Pairs well with:
Tunnel Hill Estate Pinot Noir*
Karma Vineyards Zen Red Blend
Lake Chelan Winery Reserve Syrah, Rivers Bend Estate

Jan's Crocked Duck

Duck is without question one of the tastiest of fowl. Every fall, John and our sons stock our freezer with fat, wonderful, grain-fed ducks bagged in and around North Central Washington. Even with variations in the fruit, jelly or wine, it's always a success.

Prep Time: 30 minutes
Cook Time: 5-6 hours
Serves 4-6

- 2-3 duck halves or breasts
- 1/4 cup butter
- 1 cup chopped onion
- 1/4 teaspoon tarragon
- 1/2 cup orange juice
- 1/4 teaspoon dry mustard
- 1/4 teaspoon salt
- 1/2 teaspoon rosemary
- 1/4 cup currant jelly
- 1 tablespoons grated orange rind
- 2-4 tablespoons port or burgundy wine

RECIPE TIPS

- ✦ Fruit and duck are a classic flavor combination. Try using Chelan Granny Smith apples for a different taste.
- ✦ Substitute any kind of jelly you have on hand to add the needed sweetness.
- ✦ Any dry, full-bodied red wine can be substituted for the burgundy.
- ✦ Side dishes that go well with Crocked Duck are browned potatoes, autumn squash or green salad.

Trim the excess fat and sinew from duck breasts or halves. In a sauté pan, sear the duck, breast down, in butter until golden brown. Remove ducks from pan and place breast up in crock pot. Add onions to the butter remaining in pan and sauté until tender. Add orange juice and remaining ingredients, except the wine, to the onions. Stir until jelly dissolves.

Remove from heat and add wine. Stir until well blended. Pour sauce over ducks and cook on low setting for 5-6 hours or until tender and the juices in the duck run clear.

To serve, slice the breast meat and thighs and drumsticks into smaller portions and place on platter. Drizzle extra sauce over the meat. Enjoy!

Recipe contributed by Jan Little, co-owner and assistant to the winemaker at Rio Vista Wines, page 12.

Pairs well with:
Rio Vista Estate Winery Loony Red*
Rio Vista Estate Winery Rosé*
Hard Row to Hoe Primitivo

John's Herb Baked Fish

If you are lucky enough to catch some of our Columbia River Walleye, you're fortunate indeed, because this fish dish is a delight. But Walleye isn't the only fish that makes it a hit. Try it with Halibut, Cod, Tilapia, or any firm, white fish. This tried-and-true recipe will have everyone asking for seconds. It has been a favorite of our family since the amazing True Cod days of the 1970s on Puget Sound.

Prep Time: 30 minutes
Cook Time: 10 minutes per inch of fish thickness
Serves 4-6

- 2 pounds of white fish filets (Walleye, Halibut, Cod, or Tilapia), patted dry
- 1 cup chopped sweet onion or sauté 1 cup chopped yellow onion
- 1/4 cup dry white wine
- 1 tablespoon lemon pepper
- 1/4 cup ranch dressing
- 1 tablespoon Italian seasoning
- 1/4 cup of buttered bread crumbs

Preheat oven to 400°F. Place about 1/2 cup of the chopped onion in the baking dish as a base for the filets. Pat fish dry with a paper towel. Arrange and stack filets over onion base until about one inch thick. Sprinkle the dry white wine over fish and coat lightly with lemon pepper. The ranch dressing will also add seasoning, so don't add too much!

Mix the ranch dressing, Italian seasoning, and remaining onions. Pour the mixture over fillets and spread the breadcrumbs on top of mixture. Spray top lightly with oil to help in browning and bake for about 10 to 15 minutes.

Contributed by John Little, owner and winemaker at Rio Vista Wines, page 12.

Pairs well with:
*Rio Vista Estate Chardonnay**
*Rio Vista Estate Off-Dry Riesling**
Wapato Point Cellars Pinot Grigio

RECIPE TIPS

- ✦ Contact our local fishing guides to help you locate the wily Walleye.
- ✦ View the Walleye, salmon, or Steelhead fishermen while enjoying a glass of wine on the Rio Vista deck.
- ✦ Test for freshness by smelling the fish before buying; it should not smell too fishy.
- ✦ Frozen fish is often fresher than fresh fish, as it was flash-frozen shortly after catching.
- ✦ This recipe only needs some French bread and a good wine to complete the meal; but we like to add a slice of baked yam to add color and earthy flavor.

Kentucky Bourbon Flank Steak

For best results, marinate the steak for 24 hours before cooking. Although the recipe includes instructions for broiling the flank steak, you can also flame broil or barbecue it.

Prep time: 25 minutes
Marinating time: 24 hours
Cook time: 16 minutes
Serves 2

Bourbon marinade:
- 5 tablespoons olive oil
- 2-1/2 tablespoons A-1 Steak Sauce
- 1/2 tablespoon Frank's hot sauce
- 1/2 tablespoon Worcestershire

Bourbon sauce
- 2 tablespoons Dijon mustard
- 2 tablespoons A-1 Steak Sauce
- 2 tablespoons Bourbon Whiskey
- 2 tablespoons honey

Steak seasoning
- 1 pound beef flank steak
- 1 teaspoon of your favorite steak seasoning
- ¼ cup olive oil
- 2 tablespoons dry vermouth
- ½ cup portabella mushrooms, gills and stems removed, cut into strips
- ¼ cup yellow onion, cut into strips
- ½ teaspoon whole peeled garlic
- 1 tablespoon butter

Marinate the flank steak, preferably for 24 hours. Brush the steak with oil. Diamond-score the steak, sprinkle with steak seasoning and broil (or barbecue) on each side for about 8 minutes to get a medium rare steak. Let the steak rest.

In a skillet, sauté mushrooms, onion and garlic in the olive oil and vermouth. Add the butter and the bourbon sauce. Once the butter is blended into the sauce, pour over the center of the steak. This flank steak goes well with red potatoes and fresh local asparagus.

Recipe contributed by Troy Nesvacil, chef at Campbell's Resort, page 87.

Pairs well with:
Nefarious Cellars Syrah Defiance Vineyard Lake Chelan AVA*
Tsillan Cellars Columbia Valley Bellissima Rossa Red Blend
Tunnel Hill Estate Syrah

ROAST CHICKEN AND VEGETABLES

I came up with this chicken dish after trying a similar version with pork tenderloin, which is easily interchangeable with the chicken. This is a one-pan dish that is the ultimate in easy comfort.

Prep time: 15 Minutes
Cook time: 1 hour
Serves 2

- 3 medium carrots
- 3 celery shafts
- 1 head of broccoli
- 2 small red potatoes
- 4 garlic cloves, left whole
- Salt and pepper
- 1/2 cup chicken stock
- 2 tablespoons butter
- 1 can cream of chicken soup
- 2 medium chicken breasts

RECIPE TIPS
- ✦ Substitute chicken stock with half a cup water and a cube of chicken bouillon.
- ✦ Cream of celery, cream of mushroom, or cream of potato work just as well.
- ✦ Covering the entire pan with cream of chicken soup leads to softer veggies, although they're still delicious.

Preheat oven to 350°F. Chop the vegetables into 1/2-inch pieces and place them into the bottom of a 10-inch cast iron pan. Place the whole garlic gloves in the bottom of the pan with the vegetables. Season with salt and pepper.

Pour chicken stock over vegetables. Place 1 tablespoon of butter on two opposite sides of the pan on top of the vegetables. Place chicken directly on top of the butter and season with pepper. Cover chicken with cream of chicken soup, leaving some parts of the vegetables uncovered to allow steam to escape. Place on center rack of oven and cook for one hour.

Allow dish to rest for 5 to 10 minutes before serving.

Contributed by Shane Collins, winemaker at Tsillan Cellars Winery, page 85.

Pairs well with:
*Tsillan Cellars Estate Chardonnay**
*Tsillan Cellars Estate Syrah**
Vin du Lac Vie! Viognier

Roast Duck with Blood Orange Balsalmic Fig Sauce

As my busy catering season winds down, late fall is my favorite time to relax, open a bottle of wine and cook. This recipe reflects the slow time for me and is perfect for a late October early November dinner party. Don't be afraid to cook duck. If you follow my simple instructions, it will open your world to a recipe you will love.

Prep time: 1 hour
Set time: 12 hours for chicken stock
Cook time: 3 hours 40 minutes for chicken stock; 2 hours for duck
Serves 4

- 1 whole duck (available by special order at most grocery stores)

RECIPE TIP
Blood oranges can be found in the supermarket during the late fall and winter months. It looks like a regular orange on the outside and is a beautiful dark red inside. You can find fresh-squeezed blood orange juice in the carton at Bear Foods in Chelan.

Brown Chicken Stock
(can be made up to a month in advance and frozen)
- 6 pounds chicken bones (necks, backs and any carcass pieces). Any combination of pork, beef and chicken bones you have available works for this stock, as well as the bones from the duck. To keep it simple, you can just use chicken bones.
- 1 large onion, coarsely chopped
- 2 carrots, peeled and coarsely chopped
- 4-6 cups water
- 6 whole peppercorns
- 2 bay leaves
- 1 teaspoon dried thyme leaves or several sprigs fresh thyme

Marinade
- 1 tablespoon garlic, peeled and chopped
- 1/2 cup blood orange juice
- 1 teaspoon fennel seed, ground
- 1 teaspoon cracked black pepper

Orange Balsamic Fig Sauce
- 1 cup Benson Vineyards 2007 Syrah
- 2 cups brown chicken stock
- 1/2 cup blood orange juice
- 1/4 cup Balsamic-Fig Vinegar (available at The Culinary Apple, Chelan)
- Ground fennel, salt and black pepper to your taste

Garnish
Sliced orange and/or fig

recipe continues on page 59

ROAST DUCK WITH BLOOD ORANGE
BALSALMIC FIG SAUCE (CONTINUED)

Brown Chicken Stock
Roast the bones in a 400°F oven for 20 minutes. Add the vegetables and roast for another 20 minutes. This will brown the bones and vegetables, which will add color to the stock. Place the bones and vegetables in a stock pot and cover with cold water. Heat to boiling and immediately turn down to a simmer. Skim off any scum that floats to the surface. Add the seasonings and simmer for 3 hours. Strain the bones and vegetables.

Cool the hot stock to room temperature and refrigerate overnight. In the morning, remove any solidified fat and reduce the broth by half at a slow simmer.

Marinade
Whisk the marinade ingredients together.

Duck
Remove the breast meat and legs from the duck carcass. (It is just like taking the meat off of a chicken.) Remove the fat from the breast and trim some of the fat from the legs. Do not take the bones out of the legs or remove all the fat. The legs will be roasted in the oven and the fat will keep the meat juicy. The fat also gets nice and crispy, so it will not be greasy. Place the duck legs and breast in the marinade. Turn them over every 15 minutes for an hour or two.

 Preheat the oven to 400°F. Place the legs in a baking dish (breast is cooked separately) and place in the oven. Turn the heat down to 375°F and roast for 30 minutes, until the fat is crispy on the outside. Remove from the oven.

Sauté and cook the breast meat for about 5 minutes and serve medium to medium-rare to keep it tender. Heat a sauté pan to medium-high with 1 tablespoon olive oil. When the oil is hot, sprinkle the breast with salt and pepper and place seasoned side down in the pan. Brown the breast on one side and turn it over. Brown the other side and turn the heat down to medium. Cook the breast for about 3 minutes on each side. Take the breasts out of the pan and place them in the baking dish with the legs. You will use the pan you cooked the breast in to make the sauce.

Blood Orange Balsamic Fig Sauce
Place the pan back on the heat and add the wine. This is called deglazing the pan. Scrape the bottom of the pan with a wooden spoon while the wine is reducing to remove the flavorful residue left from sautéing the breast meat. Add the broth and reduce by a third. Add the orange juice

recipe continues on page 60

ROAST DUCK WITH BLOOD ORANGE BALSALMIC FIG SAUCE (CONTINUED)

and vinegar and let the flavors cook together. Let the sauce thicken slightly and add the seasonings. Reduce a little further until the sauce coats the back of a spoon. The natural gelatin in the chicken stock will cause the sauce to have the desired consistency. To serve, spoon the sauce onto a warm plate, cut half the duck leg meat off the bone (if serving 4) and place it on the sauce. Slice half the duck breast, fan it on the plate and spoon the sauce over the breast meat. If serving two people, serve the leg whole with the bone in on the plate. Garnish with orange slices and figs.

This recipe is delicious with Gnocchi (potato dumpling), Spatzle (German noodle) or Garlic-Mashed Potatoes. The Sunshine Fruit and Vegetable Market in Chelan has a wonderful variety of fall root vegetables and leafy greens that would compliment this dish as well. For more information on the Sunshine Market, see page 14.

Contributed by Pamela Ahl, Chef and Cooking Class Instructor for Ahl Season's Catering, Amy's Manor Inn and exclusive caterer at Benson Vineyards, page 84.

Pairs well with:
C.R. Sandidge Winery Stone Tree Red Blend
Karma Vineyards Estate Pinot Noir

ROASTED SALMON

Prep time: 10 minutes
Marinating time: 1 hour
Cook time: 12 minutes
Serves 8

- 4 medium salmon fillets
- 2 tablespoons fresh lemon juice
- Orange slices
- 2 tablespoons brown sugar
- 4 teaspoons chili powder
- 2 teaspoons grated lemon rind
- 3/4 teaspoon ground cumin
- 1/2 teaspoon salt
- 1/4 teaspoon ground cinnamon

Put the salmon and lemon juice with 1 orange slice in a zip-top plastic bag; seal and marinate in refrigerator for 1 hour.

Preheat oven to 400°F or fire up the barbecue. Remove fish from the bag and discard the marinade. Combine the brown sugar, chili powder, lemon rind, cumin, salt and cinnamon in a bowl. Rub the mixture over the fish before placing in a baking dish greased with cooking oil or butter. If you are using a barbecue, wrap the fish in foil and place it on the grill. Bake for 12 minutes or until fish flakes easily when tested with a fork. Garnish with additional orange slices.

Serve with our fresh salsa on page 22, with steamed local asparagus and one of our bold red wines.

Contributed by Karl Koester, winemaker at Four Lakes Winery, page 7.

Pairs well with:
*Four Lakes Winery Trinity Red Blend**
C.R. Sandidge Winery Glam Gams Rosé
Vin du Lac Vie! Viognier

RUSSIAN STYLE SALMON

This is one of my favorite recipes; I have been serving it on and off in local restaurants for 18 years now. Originally I only used halibut, but it is very good with our Northwest wild salmon as well. Try either one.

Prep time: 15 minutes
Cook time: 12 minutes
Serves 2

- 1 cup sour cream
- 1/4 cup shredded jack and cheddar cheese
- 2 tablespoons orange juice concentrate (unfrozen)
- 1 teaspoon dried dill weed
- 1/2 teaspoon dried red chili flakes
- Two 8 oz. wild Northwest salmon fillets, without the skin (about 1 pound)
- 1/4 cup thinly sliced green onions

Preheat oven to 400°F. Mix sour cream, cheese, orange juice concentrate, dill weed and red chili flakes in a bowl. Place the salmon filets in a lightly greased casserole dish or baking pan and coat the top and sides generously with the sour cream mixture.

Bake for 12 minutes or until fish flakes easily when tested with a fork. Garnish with green onions and serve with your favorite vegetable or starch.

Recipe contributed by Troy Nesvacil, chef at Campbell's Resort, page 87.

Pairs well with:
Nefarious Cellars Viognier Defiance Vineyard Lake Chelan AVA*
Karma Vineyards Estate Pinot Noir
Wapato Point Cellars Riesling

SAUSAGE AND SUN-DRIED TOMATO POLENTA

Prep time: 35 minutes
Set time: 2-12 hours
Cook time: 10 minutes
Serves 6

> **RECIPE TIP**
> *For best results, allow the prepared polenta to set overnight before pan frying.*

- 3 cups water
- 2 cups milk (whole milk is best)
- 1-1/2 teaspoons salt
- 1-1/2 cups medium grain polenta
- 2 teaspoons chopped fresh thyme
- 1/8 teaspoon fresh ground black pepper
- 1/2 cup grated parmesan cheese
- 2 teaspoons olive oil
- 4 sliced Crimini button mushrooms
- 1/2 pound ground Italian sausage
- 1/4 cup chopped sun-dried tomatoes (in oil)

Garnish

- Freshly grated Romano and Parmesan cheeses
- 4 sliced and sautéed Crimini button mushrooms
- Chopped fresh green onions

Place the polenta in a bowl and add 1/2 cup water. In a saucepan, add the remaining water, milk and salt. Bring to a light boil, making sure the milk does not boil over. Slowly stir in the polenta. Do not cover while cooking. Lower heat enough to keep the mixture simmering. Stir every 2 to 3 minutes to prevent the mixture from sticking to the bottom of the saucepan. Cook about 30 minutes, until the mixture is very thick.

While the polenta is cooking, sauté the sausage until cooked through and add the sliced mushrooms and sun-dried tomatoes. Once the polenta has cooked 30 minutes, stir in the thyme, sausage, sun-dried tomatoes, black pepper, 1/2 cup of Parmesan cheese and mushrooms. Spoon the polenta mixture into a greased 9-1/2 inch x 5-1/2 inch bread pan. Cover with plastic wrap and refrigerate several hours, or overnight.

To serve, pop the polenta loaf out of the pan onto a cutting board and slice into 1/2 inch thick slices. Pan fry the slices in olive oil until golden brown on both sides and sauté mushrooms. Plate and garnish with freshly ground Romano and Parmesan cheeses and green onion.

Contributed by Ray Sandidge, winemaker for C. R. Sandidge Wines, page 6.

Pairs well with:
C. R. Sandidge Dry Barrel Fermented Viognier*
C. R. Sandidge Whistle Punk Red Red Blend*

SLOW COOKED FRENCH DIP

I came up with this version of French Dip because my girlfriend Melissa loves it so much, but also because I am away from the house most of the day. I use a slow cooker, but you can also bake it if you don't have one.

Prep time: 5 Minutes
Cook time: 7-8 hours
Serves 8

- About 4 pounds cheap beef roast
- 1 small can beef broth
- 1 packet dry French onion soup mix (2 oz.)
- 1 cup water
- 1 bottle dark beer
- 2 tablespoons butter
- 1 bag French Rolls
- Salt and pepper

RECIPE TIPS

✦ For more flavor, replace the water with another can of beef broth...but this can be too beefy for some.

✦ Mash garlic and rub onto the warm buttered rolls once they come off the skillet.

✦ Brown the sides of the beef roast in a skillet or pan before putting in slow cooker for more flavor and texture.

✦ If you don't have a slow cooker, bake the roast in a casserole dish or Dutch oven for 7.5 to 8 hours at 200°F.

Place whole roast in a slow cooker (Crock Pot). Leave fat on the roast for extra flavor and juiciness. Sprinkle contents from the French onion soup mix over the roast, then season with salt and pepper. Add beef broth, beer, and the cup of water to the bottom of the slow cooker around the roast. Cook on low for 7-8 hours.

Once the roast is done cooking, warm a skillet, butter the rolls and place on the skillet, butter side down, for browning. Remove the roast from the slow cooker and shred or slice the beef and put onto the warm buns. Ladle the juice or "jus" from the slow cooker into bowls and enjoy. It will be hard not to!

Contributed by Shane Collins, winemaker at Tsillan Cellars Winery, page 85.

Pairs well with:
Tsillan Cellars Estate Sinistra Red Blend*
Tsillan Cellars Columbia Valley Piccolo Rosso*
Tunnel Hill Estate Syrah

Souvlaki with Tzatziki, Pita and Fresh Vegetables

You can prepare everything but the sliced tomatoes the day before, so if you are entertaining it is very easy to prepare in advance and have little to do the night of the event. This dish goes well the Hummus on page 23 and Local Myth Greek Salad on page 34.

Prep time: 40 minutes
Marinating time: 1-12 hours
Cook time: 25 minutes
Serves 4

- 1 pork tenderloin
- 1 package pita bread
- 2 tomatoes, sliced
- 1/4 head lettuce

Marinade
- 1/2 cup red wine
- 4 cloves of garlic, pressed
- 1/8 cup olive oil

Tzatziki Sauce
- 1 cucumber, peeled, cored and grated
- 1 cup plain yogurt (best with Greek yogurt)
- 3 cloves garlic, pressed

> ### RECIPE TIP
> *Tearing lettuce instead of chopping it will keep it from going brown as quickly.*

Marinate the pork overnight or for at least one hour. The longer you marinate, the more intense the flavor. Barbecue the pork on medium heat until the outside is nice and brown: about 4 minutes per side; it will be quite red on the inside. Cool in the refrigerator for about 15 minutes. Preheat the oven to 350°F. Slice the pork into 1/4-inch rounds. Lay the rounds in a baking dish and bake for 15-20 minutes.

It is very important to core the cucumber or the Tzatziki will be very wet. Wrap the grated cucumber in a paper towel and wring it out. Add the yogurt and pressed garlic and mix together.

Rinse the lettuce, dip it in cold water, drain, wrap it in a paper towel and plastic and let it rest in the fridge for at least a half an hour to crisp. Tear into bite-sized pieces. Fill pita bread with pork, Tzatziki, tomatoes and lettuce.

Contributed by Terrie Holm-Nielsen, co-owner and designer at Columbia Furniture, page 86.

Pairs well with:
Tunnel Hill Estate Riesling
Vin du Lac "LEHM" Dry Riesling

SWEET BOURBON LAKE TROUT

Our basic grilled fish recipe is to fillet them with the skin left on. If you're barbecuing, pin the fillets in a grill grid so they don't fall apart. Grill lightly on medium heat. (We grill the fillets off of a 3-pound fish for 2 to 3 minutes per side. Thicker fillets take a little longer.)

Prep time: 15 minutes
Cook time: 20-25 minutes
Serves 2

- 1 lake trout, filleted
- 1 shot glass (2 Tbs.) Bourbon
- 2 shot glasses (4 Tbs.) brown sugar
- 1 shot glass (2 Tbs.) soy sauce

> ### RECIPE TIPS
> *Basic care instructions*
> *for local fish:*
> *1. Keep them cold*
> *2. Scrape off loose body fat*
> *3. Do not overcook*

Preheat oven to 350°F. Mix all ingredients together. The mixture should be thick; if not add a little more brown sugar.

Fillet the fish, leaving the skin on. Lay the fillet in a pan covered in tin foil to keep the drippings from ruining the pan. Pour the mixed ingredients over the fillet.

Bake for 20 to 25 minutes, or barbecue until done.

A small fish of 2 to 3 pounds will need to barbecue about 10 to 12 minutes per side on low heat. Four- to 5-pound fish need about 15 minutes per side on low heat. Six- to 7-pound fish need about 17 to 19 minutes per side on low heat.

Contributed by Anton Jones of Darrell & Dad's Family Guide Service, page 85.

Pairs well with:
Hard Row to Hoe Viognier
Lake Chelan Winery Pinot Noir
Rio Vista Viognier (Antoine Creek Vineyards)

El Vaquero Tijuana Baja Fish Tacos

Prep time: 30 minutes
Set time: 1-2 hours (optional)
Cook time: 25 minutes
Serves 6-8

RECIPE TIP
For best results, make the Pico de Gallo and Salsa Roja 1-2 hours ahead of time so the flavors can blend.

Beer Batter
- 1 cup all-purpose flour
- 1 teaspoon salt
- 1/2 teaspoon ground black pepper
- 1 cup dark Mexican beer (Negra Modelo)

Salsa Roja
- 2 medium size chiles anchos (dried poblano peppers)
- 2 cups water
- 1 tablespoon oil
- Dash salt
- 1/2 cup mayonnaise
- 1/2 cup Mexican crema (crème fraiche) or sour cream
- 1 teaspoon grated lemon zest
- 1/4 cup finely diced dill pickle
- 2 tablespoons fresh lemon juice
- 2 tablespoons water
- Salt and freshly ground black pepper

Pico de Gallo
- 2 medium tomatoes, seeded and diced
- 1/4 head of cabbage, finely chopped
- 4 green onions, thinly sliced
- 1 jalapeño, finely chopped (optional)
- 1 tablespoon lime juice
- 2 tablespoons oil
- 1 teaspoon salt
- 1 cup tomato sauce
- 1/2 bunch cilantro, chopped

Fish Tacos
- Oil, for frying
- 1 cup all-purpose flour
- 1 teaspoon salt, plus more for seasoning
- 2 pounds skinned Halibut, Cod or other white fish, cut into 1/2-inch strips
- Freshly ground black pepper
- Yellow corn tortillas (do not use white corn or flour tortillas!)
- Pickled jalapeños for garnish (optional)

recipe continues on page 69

FISH TACOS (CONTINUED)

Salsa Roja
Place the chiles in a saucepan on medium heat. Add a tablespoon of oil and lightly toast the chiles for 10-15 seconds on each side or until they change color, whichever happens first. Do not burn. Let the oil in the pan cool for about 5 minutes. Put the chiles back in the same saucepan, add water and bring to a boil. Remove from heat and let sit until softened; about 5 minutes. Grind chiles in a blender until pureed. Add some of the soaking liquid – about half a cup — to facilitate blending and to dilute the salsa to a medium-thick consistency. Add salt to bring out the flavors. Let salsa roja cool in the refrigerator for about 15 minutes.

Mix mayonnaise, crema and pickles in a medium bowl. Whisk in the lemon zest, lemon juice and water. Season to taste with salt and pepper. Add the chile mixture once it has cooled and whisk. For best results, make the sauce at least 1-2 hours ahead of time and keep it in the refrigerator until you're ready to serve the fish tacos.

For better taste and consistency, do not use an electric whisk.

Pico de Gallo
Combine ingredients in a bowl; add salt and pepper to taste. Makes 2 cups.

Beer Batter
Mix the flour, salt and pepper in a medium bowl. Gradually whisk in the beer. Set aside and let the batter rest for 15 minutes before using.

Fish
Over medium heat, add enough oil to a large skillet to reach a depth of 1 inch. Heat the oil until a deep-fry thermometer registers 350°F, or until a drop of water dances and sizzles on the oil's surface.

On a large plate, combine the flour and salt. Season the fish pieces all over with salt and pepper and coat with the flour. Working in batches, dip the fillets in the beer batter, coating both sides. Fry in the hot oil until golden brown and cooked through, about 5 minutes. Place on paper towels to drain.

For a nice semi-crispy tortilla, warm the yellow corn tortillas in a dry pan over a gas burner or grill until golden brown on both sides. Prepare tacos by filling the tortillas with fish and topping each with the salsa roja cream sauce, pico de gallo and fresh lime juice.

Contributed by JC deVivero of El Vaquero Mexican Restaurant, page 85.

Pairs well with:
Karma Vineyards Chardonnay
Nefarious Cellars Riesling Stone's Throw Vineyard Estate Grown

NOTES

Desserts

"Apricots in Summer" by Kerry Siderius

Desserts

"Apricots in Summer" by Kerry Siderius

APPLE CHIMICHANGAS

Apple Chimichangas are like homemade apple pie with a Hispanic twist. Living in North Central Washington, with it's inexhaustible supply of fruit, we're always looking for new and exciting ways to use the local bounty. A friend of mine came up with this recipe. Due to lack of time to prepare a "proper" pie or the need to use up the tortillas lingering in the refrigerator, she decided to try this delectable combination.

Prep time: 1 hour
Cook time: 15 minutes
Serves 4

- 4 apples, peeled, cored and chopped
- 1/4 cup sugar
- 1/2 teaspoon cinnamon
- 1/4 cup water
- 4 tortillas
- 3 cups vegetable oil

Garnish
- Caramel sauce, vanilla ice cream or whipped cream (recipe on page 79)

> ### RECIPE TIP
> ✦ *This recipe can be reproduced with any of the local fruits in season.*
> ✦ *Extra chimichangas can be cooled and eaten later.*
> ✦ *To produce this recipe for a larger number, use 1 apple per chimichanga and adjust sugar and cinnamon to taste.*

Stew apples, sugar, cinnamon and water in a small saucepan over medium heat until soft. Remove from heat and set aside.

In a large, high-sided pan, (I use a cast iron, Dutch oven) heat at least two inches of vegetable oil to a medium to a medium-high temperature: a drop of water shaken into the oil will dance and sizzle.

Slightly warm four flour tortillas in the microwave (about 20 seconds) until pliable. Scoop about 1/2 cup of prepared apples into the center of each tortilla and wrap securely. Gently place filled tortillas, wrapped side down, into the heated oil. Caution: the oil is hot and will sizzle as you slide the wrap in. With metal tongs handy, allow the chimichanga to fry until golden brown; rotate gently to fry the other side; each side will take about 5 minutes. When both sides are brown, move the chimichanga on to a plate lined with paper towels to absorb the excess oil. To serve, place the chimichanga on a dessert plate and serve with a scoop of vanilla ice cream and/or a drizzle of caramel sauce. You can also serve with fresh whipped cream; see recipe on page 79.

Contributed by Kasey Koski, artist and designer, page 86.

Pairs well with:
Karma Vineyards Estate Gewürtzraminer
Rio Vista Winery Sunset on the River Gewürtzraminer Pinot Grigio Blend
Wapato Point Cellars Late Harvest Riesling

AUDREY'S APPLE PIE

My grandmother grew up in Cowiche, WA, outside of Yakima. Audrey (Nana) was an amazing cook but an even better baker; she was probably making this pie from the local apples since she was very young. More than 15 years after Nana's death, the whole family still talks about the magic she created in the kitchen. We use her pie recipes at Thanksgiving and Christmas.

Prep time: 30 minutes
Cook time: 1 hour 15 minutes
Serves 8

- 2 single uncooked pie crusts
  (see Audrey's Pie Crust recipe on following page)
- 5 large Golden Delicious apples, cored, peeled and sliced
- 1 cup sugar
- 1 teaspoon cinnamon
- 3 tablespoons butter

Garnish
- Vanilla ice cream, whipped cream (see page 79) or sharp cheddar cheese

Preheat oven to 425°F. Carefully place an uncooked pie crust in a 9-inch pie pan and fill the pan with the sliced apples. Sprinkle cinnamon and sugar over the apples. Divide the butter into 10 small pieces and place them on top of the apple mixture. Roll out the second crust, place it over the apples and cut off all but about a 3/4 inch of dough around the edges. Seal the edges with your fingers or a fork.

Cut diagonal slits in top crust for venting during cooking. Brush the top of the pie with milk and sprinkle with a little sugar.

Bake for 15 minutes at 425°F. Lower the temperature to 350°F and bake for 1 hour or until top is golden brown.

Serve the pie hot with vanilla ice cream, whipped cream (see recipe on page 79) or topped with a slice of cheese.

Contributed by author Morgan Fraser, see page 98.

Pairs well with:
Lake Chelan Winery Muscat
Nefarious Cellars Consequence White Blend
Rio Vista Estate Winery Ice Wine

AUDREY'S PIE CRUST

This is the original pie crust recipe that goes with Audrey's Apple Pie on page 74. You can either pre-bake this crust for custard-filled pies or bake with the filling for fruit pies. To save time, make the dough in advance and refrigerate.

Prep time: 1 hour 30 minutes
Set time: 45 minutes to 12 hours
Cook time: 30 minutes (optional)
Makes two single crusts

RECIPE TIP
The amount of water may vary according to the elevation and humidity in your kitchen.

- 2-1/3 cups all-purpose flour
- 1 teaspoon salt
- 1 cup Crisco
- 1 egg
- 1-1/2 teaspoons cider vinegar
- 1/4 cup cold water

Combine the flour, salt and shortening in large bowl. Blend with a pastry blender, pastry cutter or knives until crumbly.

In a small bowl, whisk together the egg, cider vinegar and water. Drizzle over the flour mixture and mix thoroughly. The dough will be soft and a little sticky. If it's too sticky, add a little more flour.

Shape the dough into two patties, wrap in plastic wrap and place in the freezer for 45 minutes, or in the refrigerator overnight.

Unbaked crust
When chilled, take one patty out of the refrigerator and roll out on a floured surface. The crust should be slightly bigger than the pie pan. When you're finished with the first crust, repeat process with the second crust.

Fill the crust with the filling and bake according to the pie recipe.

Pre-baked crust
For a pre-baked crust, preheat the oven to 350°F. Press the crust firmly into the pie pan and freeze the crust until chilled, or for at least 30 minutes. This keeps the crust from slipping down the sides of the pan.

When the pie crust is chilled, line it with parchment paper, wax paper or aluminum foil. Fill the crust at least two-thirds full with weights: dry beans, rice, or stainless-steel pie weights. Bake with the weights for 20 minutes. Remove from the oven, cool for a few minutes and carefully remove pie weights. Poke holes in the bottom of the pie crust with a fork and bake for an additional 10 minutes without the weights until the crust is golden brown. Cool completely before filling. You can cover the edges of the pie with aluminum foil during baking to keep the edges from drying out or burning.

Contributed by author Morgan Fraser, see page 98.

BANANA COCONUT MACADAMIA NUT BREAD

Prep time: 20 minutes
Cook time: 1 hour
Serves 8

- 1-1/2 cups all-purpose flour
- 1/2 cup flaked coconut
- 1-1/2 teaspoons baking powder
- 1/2 teaspoon baking soda
- 1/2 teaspoon salt
- 1/2 cup chopped macadamia nuts
- 1/2 cup chocolate chips
- 2 eggs
- 3/4 cup brown sugar
- 1/2 cup vegetable oil
- 1 cup mashed ripe bananas (about 3 bananas)
- 1/2 teaspoon vanilla extract

Preheat oven to 350°F. Grease a 9"x5"x3" loaf pan.

Mix together flour, coconut, baking powder, baking soda, salt, chopped macadamia nuts and chocolate chips in a large bowl. Set aside.

Break eggs into a mixing bowl and beat until light and frothy. Add brown sugar and oil and beat well. Stir in mashed banana and vanilla. Add flour mixture and stir just until combined; do not over stir. Spoon into greased 9x5x3" loaf pan.

Bake for 1 hour, or until toothpick inserted in center comes out clean. Let stand for 10 minutes and remove from pan. The bread will cut easier if cooled completely before slicing.

Contributed by Jo Grooms, owner of Your Just Desserts, page 86.

Pairs well with:
Lake Chelan Winery Muscat
Rio Vista Winery Ice Wine
Wapato Point Cellars Late Harvest Riesling

BLUEBERRY HILLS
FARM FRESH BLUEBERRY PIE

Prep time: 5 minutes
Serves 6

RECIPE TIP
If you can't get Blueberry Hills Jam, substitute any 8 oz. jar of blueberry jam.

- One 9-inch pre-baked pie crust (see page 75)
- 3 cups fresh blueberries
- 1 jar (8 oz.) Blueberry Hills Blueberry Jam
- Fresh whipped cream (see page 79)

Toss the blueberries into pre-baked 9-inch pie shell. Heat a jar of jam (without the lid, folks!) in the microwave until it's a bit thin, about 1 minute. Pour over fresh blueberries. Let it cool before you slice it. Top with fresh whipped cream (page 79).

Now this is the important part, so pay attention:

Splash a little water on your face. Toss a handful of flour in the air and make sure to get some in your hair. (Now, really get some in there.) Head towards the living room and drape yourself haphazardly across the nearest overstuffed chair. Try to look really exhausted. Wait to be noticed. Moaning helps. You want everyone to know how much effort you went to make your pie. Ok. Enough already. Go eat your pie!

Contributed by Kari Sorensen, co-owner of Blueberry Hills Farm, page 88.

Pairs well with:
Hard Row to Hoe Edelzwicker Gewurtzraminer Riesling Blend
Lake Chelan Winery Gewürtzraminer
Tsillan Cellars Dolcezza d'Oro Estate Riesling

FRESH WHIPPED CREAM

Cream whips better if it's cold. Try putting the bowl, whisk or beaters and cream in the freezer or refrigerator for 20 minutes before starting.

Prep time: 5 minutes
Makes 2 cups

- 1 cup whipping cream or heavy cream
- 1/4 cup powdered sugar
- 1 teaspoon vanilla

Pour the cream and powdered sugar into a bowl – stainless steel works best – and whip until peaks begin to form.

If using a hand mixer, move the mixer around the bowl on a high setting. If using a whisk, put the whisk in the bowl at an angle and draw it through the cream in quick, sharp movements.

Add the vanilla while mixing. Continue to whip until the mixture is almost firm. Serve immediately.

Contributed by author Morgan Fraser, page 98.

To pair whipped cream, see pairing ideas for the dessert you're making it for.

JEANIE'S SOUR CREAM APPLE PIE

This pie is best with fresh Golden Delicious, Gravenstein, and/or Granny Smith apples. For fruit harvest dates, see page 95.

Prep time: 15 minutes
Cook time: 30 minutes
Serves 8

- One 9-inch unbaked pie shell (see page 75)

Filling
- 2/3 cup sugar
- 2 tablespoons flour
- 1/2 teaspoon salt
- 1 cup sour cream
- 1 egg
- 1/2 teaspoon vanilla
- 3/4 cup thinly sliced apple, peeled (about 1 large apple)

Topping
- 1/3 cup butter
- 1/3 cup flour
- 1/3 cup brown sugar
- 1 teaspoon cinnamon

Preheat oven to 375°F. Mix all ingredients, folding in apple slices at the end. Spoon the mixture into an unbaked pie shell. Bake at 375°F for 20 minutes, or until the pie sets.

Combine topping ingredients in a bowl and fork together until pea-sized balls form. Sprinkle the mixture over the top of the pie and bake an additional 8-10 minutes.

Contributed by Jean Haskell, co-owner of Antoine Creek Vineyard, page 5.

Pairs well with:
*Rio Vista Estate Winery Ice Wine**
Nefarious Cellars Consequence White Blend
Tsillan Cellars Estate Gewürtzraminer

NEFARIOUS CHOCOLATE TRUFFLES

This is our recipe for the truffles we make for the Red Wine and Chocolate celebration in Chelan every February. We make it with our Nefarious Cellars Syrah, but you can use any red wine, Kahlua or other liqueur. Be creative!

Prep time: 10 minutes
Set time: 1-12 hours
Cook time: 5 minutes
Makes about 20 truffles

- 7 oz. bittersweet chocolate
- 1/2 cup heavy cream
- 1-1/2 tablespoons Syrah
- 1 tablespoon coffee
- Cocoa powder

Finely chop the chocolate and place in a bowl. Heat the cream in a saucepan until it boils. Pour the hot cream over the chocolate and stir until the chocolate is completely melted. Mix in the Syrah and coffee.

Cover and chill for an hour, or until firm enough to scoop – the longer you wait, the easier this will be. Using a 1-1/4-inch ice cream scoop or melon baller, form balls and finish by rolling in cocoa powder. Truffles are best if chilled before serving.

Contributed by Heather Neff, co-owner and winemaker at Nefarious Cellars, page 11.

Pairs well with:
Nefarious Cellars Syrah Defiance Vineyard Lake Chelan AVA*
Tunnel Hill Estate Pinot Noir
Wapato Point Cellars Late Harvest Riesling

Contributors

"Strawberry Leaves Turning" by Kerry Siderius

CONTRIBUTORS

Amy's Manor

AND *Ahl Seasons Catering & Events*

Pamela Ahl, Chef and Cooking Class Instructor for Ahl Season's Catering, Amy's Manor Inn and now exclusive wedding and event caterer at Benson Vineyards

I started working in the restaurant business in the late 70's, and it sparked my love of food and wine. While most girls spent money on clothes and makeup, my roommate and I bought good bottles of wine, found the freshest ingredients at the Pike Place Market and cooked great meals in our Seattle apartment. We learned how to use wine as a base for sauces, in marinades, macerating fruit, poaching fish, glazing roast chicken and deglazing a pan sautéing beef. After attending the Culinary Institute in Hyde Park, New York, my curious exploration of the many ways that wine is used in recipes and pairing with food has continued using fruit, vegetables and wine from the local Chelan and Methow Valleys.

To contact Pam, call 509.470.1035 or go to amysmanor.com.

Amilee Cappell Olson, Chef at Karma Kafé

After graduating from culinary school fourteen years ago, my son and I moved to Washington from southern California. I apprenticed at the historic Wenatchee restaurant, The John Horan House. I moved from there to a personal chef business, to working as a resort chef and catering chef. I came to Karma Vineyards two and half years ago. My passion is not only for food and cooking; it is sharing my love and passion of food and cooking with others.

For more information about Karma Kafe at Karma Vineyards, see page 9.

Shane Collins, Head Winemaker/Viticulturist at Tsillan Cellars

Shane Collins is a native of the Lake Chelan Valley and a fourth generation orchardist. After receiving a B.A. in Communication from Washington State University, his interests in farming and agriculture brought him back to the valley to pursue the field of viticulture and grape growing. Shane studied viticulture and fermentation science at the Institute of Enology and Viticulture. He is now the winemaker at Tsillan Cellars. There was never any doubt that he would spend his life in the Lake Chelan Valley. He considers himself very fortunate to work in agriculture in such a beautiful place that his great grandparents settled in nearly 75 years ago. "I never considered myself the city type. Working with crops is often a very humbling experience and there is nothing more satisfying to me than crafting wines from the ground up. I am truly blessed to work in such great award-winning vineyards. At times I seem like no more than a baby sitter to wines that almost craft themselves."

See Tsillan Cellars on page 13 or email Shane at shane@tsillancellars.com.

Darrell and Dad's Family Guide Service

Darrell and Dad's is a family-oriented fishing guide service on Lake Chelan, Rufus Woods Reservoir, the Columbia River for steelhead and salmon as well as little Roses Lake. We also provide family lodging. Multiple boat trips can be arranged.

Go to darrellanddads.com, email antonj@aol.com or call 509.687.0709.

El Vaquero Mexican Restaurant

The Viveros Family welcomes you to El Vaquero Restaurant. We pride ourselves in having our own vegetable garden and trading with local growers, making us 90% sustainable in our produce and sauces. Come try a taste of homemade recipes from the Guerrero Region.

Visit El Vaquero at 75 W. Wapato Way in Manson or call 509.687.3179.

CONTRIBUTORS (CONTINUED)

Jo Grooms, Owner of Your Just Desserts

Jo Grooms is the owner of Your Just Desserts, a small cupcake, dessert and coffee shop in Chelan. Your Just Desserts specializes in freshly baked cupcakes, with flavors like Lemonaholic, Espresso Yourself and Red Velvet, together with other decadent dessert items.

Visit Jo at 110 E Woodin Avenue in Chelan, call 509.888.5335 or go to justdessertsshop.com

Terrie Holm-Nielsen, Co-owner and Designer at Columbia Furniture

My interest in food and cooking was sparked on a two-year trek through Western Europe. I was intrigued by how different cultures used the same ingredients in different ways. My love of cooking is still strong today. There is always more to learn and more good recipes to try, both of which helped me in the catering company I owned before becoming a designer at Columbia Furniture. Bon Apetit!

To contact Terrie, call 509.682.9007 or go to columbiafurniture.com.

Kasey Koski, Artist, Designer and Domestic Adventurer

Creativity has always been a driving force in my life and that doesn't stop short of the kitchen. A love for fresh, local food has inspired me to become an urban gardener and supplier for a local restaurant. This summer's goal is to master canning. Next, who knows?

To contact Kasey, email her at kaseykoski@yahoo.com.

Troy Nesvacil, Chef at Campbell's Bistro and Pub

Delicious, cravable flavors. Seasonal, boldly-flavored fare, prepared with rustic simplicity and delivered with over-the-top hospitality. Featuring au fresco dining and Wine Press Northwest Magazine's 'Best Washington Wine List.'

Campbell's Bistro and Pub are located in the original landmark Campbell Hotel in downtown Chelan. Serving breakfast, lunch and dinner.

Visit Campbell's Bistro and Pub at 104 W. Woodin Ave. in Chelan. Call 509.682.4250 or go to dineatcampbells.com.

Kerry Siderius, Watercolor Artist

Kerry Siderius was raised an apple orchardist's daughter on a small farm in Bridgeport, WA. Their apple farm sat along the beautiful banks of the Columbia where Canada geese, salmon and apples were plentiful. Kerry began painting her surroundings at three years old and she's never stopped.

To see more of Kerry's work, visit her gallery in the tasting room at Rio Vista Wines (see page 12) or go to kerrysiderius.com. To order a painting, email kerry@kerrysiderius.com.

Art Sill, Co-owner of Local Myth Pizza

Before opening the restaurant 13 years ago, Art Sill sold take-and-bake pizzas from his home. Before long, many people had tried his pizzas, but not everyone could figure out where to buy them. This mythical reputation and Art's love for anything local brought about the name Local Myth. Art and his daughter Brittany run the restaurant with the help of their dedicated staff.

Visit Local Myth at 122 S. Emerson St. in Chelan or call 509.682.2914.

CONTRIBUTORS (CONTINUED)

Kari Sorensen, Co-owner and General Manager at Blueberry Hills Farms

Kari is known for down-home, scratch country cooking and her eccentric sense of humor.

Visit Blueberry Hills at 1315 Washington Street in Manson, call 509.687.2379 or go to wildaboutblueberries.com.

Rich Uhlhorn, Photographer

Richard Uhlhorn has been a professional photographer and journalist in the Lake Chelan Valley since 1988. He has enjoyed the new adventure in food photography that *Savoring Chelan* has provided.

Contact Richard at 509.682.0602, richard@richarduhlhorn.com, or go to richarduhlhorn.com.

Mary Weldy, Co-owner of The Culinary Apple

The Culinary Apple is a combination of The Harvest Tree and the Kitchen Station stores in downtown Chelan. We have been family owned since 1996 by Mary and David Weldy. The store features kitchen and gift items with above-and-beyond customer service.

Come see us 7 days a week at 109 E. Woodin Avenue in Chelan, call 509.682.3618 or 800.568.6062, or go to culinaryapple.com.

Index

"Gala Apple, Yellow Leaves" by Kerry Siderius

INDEX ~ CONTRIBUTORS

Photography and Design

Pictures on winery pages belong to the wineries unless otherwise noted.

Recipe Contributors

Watercolor Paintings

Bold page numbers mark the information page about the contributor
and include their contact information.

INDEX ~ RECIPES BY NAME

Index ~ Wines by Winery

INDEX ~ WINES BY WINERY (CONTINUED)

CHELAN FRUIT HARVEST DATES

Apples	May	June	July	Aug.	Sept.	Oct.
Braeburn						X
Fuji					X	X
Gala				X	X	
Gingergold				X		
Golden Delicious					X	X
Granny Smith						X
Honey Crisp					X	
Jonagold					X	X
Pink Lady						X
Red Delicious					X	X

Berries	May	June	July	Aug.	Sept.	Oct.
Blackberries		X	X	X		
Blueberries		X	X			
Raspberries		X	X	X		

Cherries	May	June	July	Aug.	Sept.	Oct.
Bing	X	X				
Chelan		X	X			
Lapin		X	X			
Montmorency		X				
Rainier	X	X				
Sweetheart		X	X			

Peaches	May	June	July	Aug.	Sept.	Oct.
Cresthaven				X	X	
Donut			X	X		
Elberta					X	
O'Henry				X	X	
Red Globe				X	X	
Red Haven				X		

Pears	May	June	July	Aug.	Sept.	Oct.
Asian					X	
Bartlett				X	X	
Bosc					X	
D'Anjou					X	

Other Fruits	May	June	July	Aug.	Sept.	Oct.
Apricots			X			
Nectarines			X	X		
Plumcots			X	X		

Note: Harvest varies yearly based on weather; these are estimates only.

CHELAN VALLEY VISITOR'S INFORMATION

Lodging, Tourism and Wine-Tasting Information

Lake Chelan Chamber of Commerce
102 East Johnson Avenue
Chelan, WA 98816
509.682.3503
lakechelan.com

Lake Chelan Tourism Promotion Group
877.440.7933
cometothelake.com

Lake Chelan Wine Grape Grower's Association
lakechelanwinevalley.com

Historic Downtown Chelan Association
historicchelan.org
509.682.4322

News and Community Information

KOZI Community Radio ~ 100.9 FM
509.682.4033
kozi.com

Lake Chelan Mirror Newspaper
509.682.2213
lakechelanmirror.com

GoLakeChelan.com
509.888.5253

ACKNOWLEDGEMENTS

Savoring Chelan is a collaboration, and I would like to thank everyone who made this book possible.

Thank you to Jennie and Myrna Simpson, who gave me insight on how to approach the wineries with my idea of pairing their wines with favorite local recipes. I would also like to thank Don Phelps for being the first to sit down with me and figure out where the idea might go.

Thank you to Shane Collins and John and Jan Little for being key to the process — freely giving of their time, energy, expertise and connections — to make the book what it is.

Thank you to my recipe testers, who gave honest feedback and made sure everything was perfect: Angela Berg, Laurie Davidson, Barbie Guzmán, Anna Koenig, Emily McLean, Kim Rothlisberger, Sarah Sluis, and especially Megan Albrecht, for testing over and over again and always sending thorough feedback.

Thank you to my writer's group: Molly Steere, Yvette Davis, Nancy Jarmin, Anita Van Stralen and Nancy Trucano, for cheering me on, giving me feedback and testing my recipes.

Thank you Beckie Frame, Elisha Grange, Nancy Trucano, Anita Van Stralen and Rose Weagant Norton for editing the book into some semblance of order and making it accessible to readers and cooks alike.

Thank you to all 27 recipe contributors and winery owners who took the time to gather the materials and answer my emails. There wouldn't be a book without you.

Thank you especially to graphic designer Kasey Koski, watercolor artist Kerry Siderius and photographer Richard Uhlhorn; your contributions made *Savoring Chelan* colorful and appetizing.

And thank you most of all to my parents, Janet and Stu, for eating everything I put in front of them, listening patiently to my incessant chatter about the project, and for always telling me I could achieve whatever I put my mind to.

ABOUT THE AUTHOR

Photo by Richard Uhlhorn

Morgan Fraser is a Chelan Valley native whose travel addiction has taken her all over the world in search of new adventures, foods and flavors to pair with wine.

Morgan attended Manson High School and grew up on an apple orchard, where she learned to differentiate between store-bought off-season apples and the unmistakable flavor of fresh-picked fruit. Heavily steeped in the apple farming culture, Morgan reached royalty status when she was crowned Manson Apple Blossom Princess in 2000. Although the title was passed on years ago, Morgan still considers herself an apple aficionado.

Morgan attended Washington State University and studied abroad for a year in Spain, where her love for travel – and wine – began to develop. After graduating with degrees in journalism and Spanish, she lived, traveled and worked in many countries and several states. Despite all her time abroad, however, Morgan has never been able to call anywhere but the Chelan Valley home.

Currently Morgan divides her time between Eastern Washington and Mexico. She spends her time writing fiction, non-fiction and travelogues and creating incredibly spicy fusion dishes.